SALADS

BRIMAR

Editor Angela Rahaniotis
Graphic Design Zapp
Photography Marc Bruneau
Food Preparation / Stylist Josée Robitaille
Assistant Stylist Marc Maula
Tableware courtesy of Stokes and Hutschenreuter

©1994 Brimar Publishing Inc.
338 Saint Antoine St. East
Montreal, Canada H2Y 1A3
Tel.: (514) 954-1441
Fax: (514) 954-5086

ISBN 2-89433-161-4
Printed in Canada

SALADS

Summer or winter, salads add a note of
garden freshness and an element of easy
sophistication to mealtime.

With this collection of recipes, you will find
new and intriguing ways to present standard
salad ingredients as well as the more
exotic offerings from your greengrocer.

You will discover interesting starters such as
Cold Purée of Aubergine Salad, and a superb
selection of salad side dishes based
on simple, yet unusual ingredients such
as beetroot and citrus fruits. You will also
discover some exciting main courses,
including Curried Prawns and Rice Salad,
and Fresh Halibut Salad.

We have also included 16 easy recipes
for salad dressings and mayonnaises that are
sure to become family favourites.

Salads are a wonderful way to express your
creativity. So use this cookbook as your guide
to a fresh look at salads. And enjoy!

WATERCRESS

CABBAGE LETTUCE

LAMB'S LETTUCE

ROMAINE LETTUCE

ENDIVE

CHICORY HEADS

RADICCIO

SPINACH

ESCAROLE

RED LEAF LETTUCE

DANDELION LEAVES

Choosing and Preparing Ingredients for Salads

•

It is important that the freshest of ingredients be used in salads. Choose vegetables that are in season and ripe.

•

All greens must be washed in plenty of cold water to remove grit and sand. Dry thoroughly, using a spin-type salad dryer, if available. Watery greens will prevent the dressing from adhering properly.

•

Some salads require time to marinate, others may be served immediately. Unless indicated, salads are best served at room temperature.

How to Peel and Seed Tomatoes

1 Core tomatoes and make an X-shaped incision on the base.

2 Plunge in boiling water just long enough to loosen skins.

3 Remove from water and let cool. Peel off skins.

4 Cut tomatoes in half horizontally, or into quarters or slices. Squeeze out seeds and juice. Chop tomato flesh and prepare to use.

Apple Cole Slaw
(4 to 6 servings)

1	small head cabbage, cored	1
2	apples, cored	2
1	carrot, peeled and grated	1
½	small onion, grated	½
50 ml	mayonnaise	2 fl oz
50 ml	plain yogurt	2 fl oz
15 ml	French mustard	1 tbsp
	salt and white pepper	
	pinch of sugar	
	oil and vinegar to taste	

1 Cut cabbage into four and slice thinly. Place in large bowl. Peel apples and cut into julienne. Add to bowl.

2 Add remaining ingredients, except oil and vinegar, and mix very well.

3 Correct seasoning. Add oil and vinegar to taste. Mix and marinate 30 minutes before serving.

Spicy Creamy Cole Slaw
(4 to 6 servings)

125 ml	soured cream	4 fl oz
125 ml	mayonnaise	4 fl oz
10 ml	English mustard	2 tsp
15 ml	cider vinegar	1 tbsp
15 ml	horseradish	1 tbsp
1	head white cabbage, cored and shredded	1
1	carrot, peeled and grated	1
15 ml	chopped fresh parsley	1 tbsp
	salt and freshly ground pepper	
	lemon juice to taste	

1 Place soured cream, mayonnaise, mustard, vinegar, salt, pepper and lemon juice in bowl. Mix together. Stir in horseradish.

2 Place remaining ingredients in large bowl. Add dressing and mix well. Cover with cling film and chill at least 4 hours before serving.

Red Leaf Lettuce Salad with Radishes
(4 servings)

I	head red leaf lettuce	I
I	small head Boston lettuce	I
6	radishes, cleaned and thinly sliced	6
30 g	toasted pine nuts	I oz
30 ml	French mustard	2 tbsp
75 ml	double cream	2½ fl oz
	salt and black pepper	
	cayenne pepper to taste	
	lemon juice to taste	

1 Wash lettuce in plenty of cold water and dry thoroughly. Tear leaves into small pieces and place in large bowl. Add radishes and pine nuts.

2 Place mustard, salt, black pepper, cayenne pepper and lemon juice in small bowl. Whisk in cream gradually.

3 Pour dressing over salad, toss and serve.

Rice Salad with Crabmeat
(4 to 6 servings)

375 g	cooked rice	13 oz
225 g	cooked crabmeat	1/2 lb
1	sweet red pepper, peeled and diced	1
120 g	chopped pimiento pepper	4 oz
1/2	celery stick, diced	1/2
135 g	stoned black olives	4 1/2 oz
2	hard-boiled eggs	2
30 ml	wine vinegar	2 tbsp
5 ml	French mustard	1 tsp
90 ml	olive oil	3 fl oz
15 ml	chopped fresh parsley	1 tbsp
	salt and pepper	
	lettuce leaves	

1 Place rice, crabmeat, red pepper, pimiento pepper, celery and olives in large bowl. Season well and set aside.

2 Slice hard-boiled eggs in half and remove yolks. Reserve whites for other uses.

3 Place yolks in bowl with vinegar. Mash until smooth, then add mustard. Mix well. Incorporate oil and season well. Add parsley and pour dressing over salad. Toss until thoroughly coated. Serve on lettuce leaves.

Pineapple Rice Salad
(4 to 6 servings)

225 g	steamed rice	½ lb
150 g	diced fresh pineapple	5 oz
200 g	sectioned grapefruit	7 oz
50 ml	double cream	2 fl oz
	juice of 1 lemon	
	salt and white pepper	
	pinch of paprika	

1 Mix all ingredients together until well blended. Correct seasoning.

2 Serve salad on bed of lettuce and decorate with fresh chervil, if desired.

Waldorf Salad
(4 to 6 servings)

2	large apples, cored, peeled and cut into julienne	2
1	celeriac, peeled and cut into julienne	1
125 ml	light mayonnaise	4 fl oz
30 ml	soured cream	2 tbsp
15 ml	chopped fresh parsley	1 tbsp
15 ml	chopped fresh tarragon	1 tbsp
	juice of 1 lemon	
	French mustard to taste	
	salt and white pepper	
	cayenne pepper to taste	

1 Place apples and celeriac in large bowl. Cover with cold water and add lemon juice. Let stand 2 hours.

2 Drain well and squeeze out excess water. Place apples and celeriac in bowl.

3 Mix mayonnaise and soured cream together. Add mustard to taste. Stir into salad until evenly coated. Add fresh herbs and seasonings. Mix well.

4 Serve on bed of lettuce leaves.

Easy Salmon Salad
(4 servings)

600 g	fresh salmon, cooked, boned and flaked	1 1/4 lb
1	celery stick, diced	1
2	shallots, peeled and chopped	2
3	spring onions, chopped	3
1	hard-boiled egg, chopped	1
50 ml	mayonnaise	2 fl oz
	salt and pepper	
	juice of 1 lemon	

1 Place salmon and vegetables in bowl. Add hard-boiled egg, mayonnaise, salt and pepper. Mix well.

2 Add lemon juice and mix again. Correct seasoning and serve on mixed greens. Garnish with slices of cooked mushrooms, if desired.

Cooked Vegetable Salad with Creamy Dressing
(6 servings)

I	large potato, boiled, peeled and diced	I
225 g	French beans, cooked and diced	½ lb
90 g	cooked green peas	3 oz
175 g	cooked white beans	6 oz
I	bunch fresh asparagus, cooked and diced	I
I	small head cauliflower, cooked	I
125 ml	mayonnaise	4 fl oz
45 ml	soured cream	3 tbsp
	salt and freshly ground black pepper	
	paprika and cayenne pepper to taste	
	juice of 1 lemon	
	lettuce leaves	
	chopped fresh parsley	

1 Place all vegetables, except cauliflower, in large bowl. Season well and incorporate ¾ of mayonnaise and 30 ml (2 tbsp) of soured cream. Add half of lemon juice, mix well and correct seasoning.

2 Arrange salad on bed of lettuce, shaping cavity in middle.

3 Divide cauliflower into florets and place in bowl. Add remaining mayonnaise, soured cream and lemon juice. Season well and mix together. Add paprika, cayenne pepper and chopped parsley to taste.

4 Place cauliflower in cavity created by vegetable salad.

Spaghettini Salad with Salmon Caviar
(4 servings)

225 g	spaghettini	½ lb
30 ml	chopped fresh chives	2 tbsp
1	shallot, peeled and chopped	1
15 ml	extra virgin olive oil	1 tbsp
30 ml	salmon caviar	2 tbsp
	salt and freshly ground pepper	

1 Cook spaghettini in boiling, salted water until al dente. Drain well and transfer to large bowl.

2 Add chives, shallot and olive oil. Toss and season well.

3 Serve salad with salmon caviar.

Fresh Mussel Salad with Balsamic Vinaigrette
(4 servings)

45 ml	balsamic vinegar	3 tbsp
15 ml	French mustard	1 tbsp
1	garlic clove, peeled, crushed and chopped	1
15 ml	chopped fresh tarragon	1 tbsp
175 ml	olive oil	6 fl oz
12	prawns, peeled and deveined	12
12	fresh mussels, steamed and shelled	12
1	salmon steak, cooked and flaked	1
10	French beans, cooked	10
10	yellow beans, cooked	10
1	roasted sweet yellow pepper, skinned and thinly sliced	1
12	stoned black olives	12
	salt and pepper	
	lemon juice to taste	
	lettuce leaves	

1 Place vinegar, mustard, garlic and tarragon in small bowl. Season well. Add 135 ml (4½ fl oz) of olive oil and whisk together to incorporate. Add lemon juice to taste and set aside.

2 Heat remaining oil in frying pan over medium heat. Add prawns to hot pan and continue cooking over high heat for 3 minutes. Season well. Transfer prawns to large bowl.

3 Add cooked mussels and salmon to bowl containing prawns. Cut French and yellow beans into 2.5-cm (1-in) pieces and add to bowl. Toss in roasted sweet pepper and olives.

4 Season generously and pour in vinaigrette. Mix well and serve over lettuce leaves.

Julienne Luncheon Salad
(4 to 6 servings)

1	small head romaine lettuce, washed and dried	1
1	head cabbage lettuce, washed and dried	1
3	beetroots, boiled and peeled	3
1	celery stick	1
4	spring onions	4
2	small tomatoes, cored and cut in wedges	2
15 ml	chopped fresh basil	1 tbsp
15 ml	chopped fresh parsley	1 tbsp
125 ml	Mustard Vinaigrette (see p. 86)	4 fl oz
	salt and pepper	

1 Shred lettuces and arrange on each plate.

2 Cut beetroots, celery and spring onions into sticks. Place in large bowl, add herbs and season with salt and pepper. Pour in vinaigrette and toss.

3 Spoon vegetables in the middle of lettuce. Arrange tomatoes decoratively on lettuce.

4 Garnish with fresh basil leaves, if desired, and serve immediately.

Salad Niçoise
(4 to 6 servings)

I	head cabbage lettuce, washed and dried	I
225 g	French beans, blanched	½ lb
I	sweet green pepper, thinly sliced	I
I	sweet yellow pepper, thinly sliced	I
2	tomatoes, cored, peeled and cut in narrow wedges	2
I	small red onion, peeled and cut in rings	I
200 g	solid white tuna	7 oz
30 g	stoned black olives	I oz
50 ml	Basic Vinaigrette (see p. 89)	2 fl oz
5	anchovy fillets, drained and chopped	5
3	hard-boiled eggs, quartered	3
	juice of I lemon	
	salt and freshly ground pepper	

1 Tear lettuce leaves into small pieces and place in large salad bowl. Add some of lemon juice, toss and set aside.

2 Place vegetables, tuna and olives in separate bowl. Season well and pour in vinaigrette. Mix well.

3 Spoon mixture over lettuce in bowl. Decorate with anchovies and hard-boiled eggs. Add lemon juice to taste and serve.

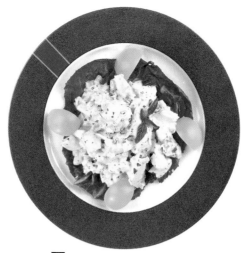

Fresh Halibut Salad

(4 servings)

1	onion, peeled and sliced	1
1	celery stick, sliced	1
1	carrot, peeled and sliced	1
1	bay leaf	1
3	fresh parsley sprigs	3
12	black peppercorns	12
250 ml	dry white wine	8 fl oz
700 g	fresh halibut	1 1/2 lb
	salt and pepper / lemon juice	

1 Place 1.5 litres (2½ pt) water in roasting tin. Add remaining ingredients, except halibut, and bring to boiling point over high heat.

2 Reduce heat to low and add halibut. Cook 8 to 10 minutes or adjust time according to thickness. When done, remove from liquid and let cool.

1	celery stick, diced	1
2	shallots, peeled and chopped	2
1/2	cucumber, peeled, seeded and diced	1/2
15 ml	chopped fresh parsley	1 tbsp
5 ml	chopped fresh chives	1 tsp
45 ml	mayonnaise	3 tbsp
	cooked fresh halibut	
	few drops of Tabasco sauce	
	salt and pepper / lemon juice	

1 Carefully bone and flake halibut. Place in large bowl. Add vegetables, fresh herbs and seasonings. Mix together gently.

2 Add mayonnaise and mix well. Squeeze in lemon juice and mix again. Correct seasoning and add more mayonnaise, if desired.

3 Serve salad on bed of radiccio leaves and garnish with wedges of yellow or red tomato, if desired.

Summer Salad
(4 to 6 servings)

3	potatoes, boiled and peeled	3
3	celery sticks	3
3	tomatoes, cored, peeled, seeded and sliced	3
I	small red onion, peeled and sliced in rings	I
2	hard-boiled eggs, sliced	2
	salt and pepper	
	Mustard Vinaigrette (see p. 86)	

1 Slice potatoes and celery into julienne. Place in bowl with tomatoes. Season well with salt and pepper.

2 Pour in vinaigrette to taste and mix well. Marinate 30 minutes before serving.

3 Decorate portions with rings of red onion and slices of hard-boiled egg.

Hot Black Bean and Scallop Salad
(4 servings)

2	garlic cloves, peeled, crushed and chopped	2
45 ml	wine vinegar	3 tbsp
15 ml	chopped fresh tarragon	1 tbsp
50 ml	olive oil	2 fl oz
450 g	fresh scallops, cleaned	1 lb
1	tin (540 ml/19 oz) black beans, drained and rinsed	1
1	head cabbage lettuce, washed and dried	1
	salt and black pepper	
	cayenne pepper to taste	
	chopped fresh parsley	

1 Mix garlic with vinegar, tarragon and oil. Season generously and pour half of mixture in frying pan. Set remaining vinaigrette aside.

2 Heat frying pan over medium heat. When vinaigrette is hot, add scallops and cook 1 minute on each side or adjust time according to size. Using slotted spoon, remove scallops and set aside in bowl.

3 Heat remaining vinaigrette in frying pan. Add black beans and cayenne pepper to taste; cook 3 minutes over high heat. Add beans to bowl containing scallops.

4 Tear lettuce leaves into small pieces and place in large bowl. Add scallops and black beans, toss and correct seasoning.

5 Sprinkle with chopped parsley and serve.

Hearty Lobster and Vegetable Salad
(6 servings)

1	head romaine lettuce	1
450 g	cooked lobster meat, chopped	1 lb
350 g	fresh asparagus, cooked and cut in 2.5-cm (1-in) pieces	¾ lb
225 g	fresh mushrooms*, cleaned, cooked and halved	½ lb
12	water chestnuts, halved	12
12	cherry tomatoes, cored	12
125 ml	mayonnaise	4 fl oz
125 ml	Ranch Dressing (see p. 95)	4 fl oz
45 ml	chilli sauce	3 tbsp
5 ml	French mustard	1 tsp
	salt and freshly ground pepper	
	lemon juice to taste	
	Tabasco sauce to taste	

1 Wash lettuce in plenty of cold water. Drain well and dry thoroughly. Tear leaves into small pieces.

2 Place lobster, asparagus, mushrooms, water chestnuts and cherry tomatoes in large bowl. Season well.

3 Add lettuce and toss ingredients.

4 Mix mayonnaise, Ranch Dressing, chilli sauce and mustard together. Add lemon juice and Tabasco sauce to taste; mix well.

5 Pour dressing over salad and toss well. Serve.

*Refer to Cooking Mushrooms for Salads (page 83).

Warm Mussel and Potato Salad
(4 servings)

2 kg	fresh mussels, bearded and scrubbed	4½ lb
2	shallots, peeled and chopped	2
125 ml	dry white wine	4 fl oz
350 g	diced, boiled potatoes, still warm	¾ lb
½	celery stick, diced	½
15 ml	chopped fresh parsley	1 tbsp
2	spring onions, chopped	2
125 ml	mayonnaise	4 fl oz
	salt and freshly ground pepper	
	lemon juice to taste	
	few drops of Tabasco sauce	

1 Place mussels, shallots and wine in large pot. Season with pepper. Cover and bring to boil. Cook mussels over low heat until shells open, about 5 minutes. Stir once during cooking.

2 Remove mussels from pot, discarding any unopened shells. Remove mussels from opened shells and place in large bowl.

3 Add remaining ingredients to bowl and season well. Mix and serve on lettuce leaves with slices of lemon.

Green Salad with Gruyère Cheese
(4 servings)

2	heads romaine lettuce, washed and dried	2
2	chicory heads, cored, washed and dried	2
2	hard-boiled eggs, sliced	2
2	anchovy fillets, drained and puréed	2
45 ml	wine vinegar	3 tbsp
I	shallot, peeled and chopped	I
135 ml	olive oil	4 1/2 fl oz
3	anchovy fillets, drained and chopped	3
100 g	grated Gruyère cheese	3 1/2 oz
	salt and pepper	
	juice of 1/2 lemon	

1 Tear lettuce and chicory into small pieces. Place in large bowl with sliced eggs. Season well.

2 Place puréed anchovy fillets in small bowl. Add vinegar, shallot, salt and pepper. Mix well. Add oil and whisk to incorporate.

3 Pour dressing over salad and toss together. Add lemon juice and toss again. Add chopped anchovies, mix and serve. Sprinkle portions with grated cheese. Garnish with lamb's lettuce and basil, if desired.

Salad of Chicory, Potatoes and Pork
(4 servings)

4	large chicory heads	4
4	potatoes, boiled, peeled and sliced	4
90 ml	olive oil	3 fl oz
1	smoked pork cutlet, sliced	1
15 ml	French mustard	1 tbsp
1	shallot, peeled and chopped	1
30 ml	balsamic vinegar	2 tbsp
15 ml	chopped fresh parsley	1 tbsp
	salt and pepper	
	juice of ½ lemon	

1 Core chicory heads and separate leaves. Wash well in cold water, drain and dry thoroughly. Place in large bowl with potatoes.

2 Heat a few drops of oil in frying pan over medium heat. When hot, add smoked pork and stir-fry 2 minutes. Add pork to bowl. Season with salt and pepper.

3 In small bowl, place mustard, shallot, salt and pepper. Add vinegar and remaining oil; mix together with whisk. Add parsley and lemon juice; mix again.

4 Pour dressing over salad, toss well and serve.

Avocado Salad with French Beans and Olives
(4 servings)

45 ml	lime juice	3 tbsp
50 ml	olive oil	2 fl oz
3	garlic cloves, blanched and puréed	3
5 ml	celery seeds	1 tsp
1	large avocado, peeled, stoned and sliced	1
1	small cucumber, peeled, seeded and cut into julienne	1
1	sweet green pepper, cut into julienne	1
1	sweet red pepper, cut into julienne	1
225 g	French beans, cooked and halved	1/2 lb
75 g	stoned black olives	2 1/2 oz
	pinch of cumin	
	pinch of sugar	
	salt and pepper	

1 Mix lime juice with oil, garlic and celery seeds. Add pinch of cumin and sugar; season well. Whisk to incorporate.

2 Place remaining ingredients in large bowl. Season well. Pour in dressing, toss together and serve.

3 Sprinkle with chopped fresh parsley, if desired.

Romaine Salad with Grilled Chicken
(4 servings)

2	heads romaine lettuce, washed and dried	2
30 g	croutons	1 oz
15 ml	soy sauce	1 tbsp
15 ml	olive oil	1 tbsp
2	garlic cloves, blanched and puréed	2
1	whole boneless chicken breast	1
125 ml	Ranch Dressing (see p. 95)	4 fl oz
60 g	grated Parmesan cheese	2 oz
	salt and pepper	

1 Tear lettuce leaves into small pieces and place in large bowl. Add croutons, season well and set aside.

2 Mix soy sauce with oil and garlic. Skin chicken and split into halves. Brush mixture over chicken and season well with pepper.

3 Cook chicken in preheated grill 10 minutes or adjust time according to size. Turn breasts over once during grilling.

4 Add Ranch Dressing to greens and mix well. Divide among dinner plates.

5 Slice grilled chicken on the bias and arrange on lettuce. Sprinkle with cheese and serve at once.

Tossed Greens with Grated Carrot
(4 to 6 servings)

1	head endive	1
1	bunch watercress	1
3	chicory heads, cored	3
125 ml	Ranch Dressing (see p. 95)	4 fl oz
45 g	garlic croutons	1 ½ oz
30 ml	grated Parmesan cheese	2 tbsp
1	large carrot, peeled and grated	1
1	apple, cored, peeled and cut into julienne	1
	salt and pepper	

1 Wash endive, watercress and chicory separately in cold water. Drain well and dry thoroughly. Tear endive into small pieces and place in large bowl with watercress.

2 Pour in dressing and toss until evenly coated. Season with salt and pepper. Toss again.

3 Add croutons and cheese, mix and divide among plates. Arrange carrot, apple and chicory decoratively on greens. Serve.

Cauliflower and Grated Carrot Salad
(4 to 6 servings)

1	cauliflower, blanched	1
2	carrots, peeled and grated	2
175 ml	mayonnaise	6 fl oz
30 ml	soured cream	2 tbsp
5 ml	French mustard	1 tsp
15 ml	chopped fresh parsley	1 tbsp
	salt and pepper	
	pinch of paprika	
	lemon juice to taste	

1 Divide cauliflower into florets and place in large bowl. Add carrots, season and mix.

2 In small bowl, mix mayonnaise with soured cream and mustard. Add dressing to salad and mix well.

3 Season with salt, pepper and paprika. Add lemon juice to taste. Sprinkle with parsley and serve.

Stuffed Tomato Salad
(4 servings)

4	large tomatoes	4
225 g	fresh prawns, cooked, peeled, deveined and finely chopped	½ lb
I	shallot, peeled and finely chopped	I
15 ml	chopped fresh parsley	1 tbsp
I	celery stick from celery heart, finely chopped	I
45 ml	mayonnaise	3 tbsp
5 ml	French mustard	1 tsp
I	bunch watercress, washed and dried	I
50 ml	Mustard Vinaigrette (see p. 86)	2 fl oz
	salt and pepper	
	lemon juice to taste	

1 Core tomatoes and slice off tops. Scoop out most of flesh and reserve for other uses. Season inside of tomatoes well.

2 Place prawns, shallot, parsley and celery in bowl. Add mayonnaise and mustard; mix well. Season and add lemon juice to taste.

3 Stuff tomatoes with prawn salad. Place tomatoes on serving platter or dinner plates and surround with watercress. Drizzle vinaigrette over watercress and serve.

Baked Beetroot Salad
(4 servings)

5	large beetroots, cleaned	5
½	red onion, finely chopped	½
15 ml	chopped fresh parsley	1 tbsp
5 ml	chopped fresh tarragon	1 tsp
30 ml	French mustard	2 tbsp
1	garlic clove, blanched and puréed	1
1	shallot, peeled and chopped	1
75 ml	double cream	2½ fl oz
	juice of 1 lemon	
	salt and freshly ground pepper	

1 Preheat oven to 190°C (375°F) mark 5.

2 Place beetroots in baking tin. Bake 40 minutes in oven or adjust time according to size. Test if beetroots are cooked by inserting paring knife (the same way you would for potatoes). Flesh should be soft with no resistance.

3 Let beetroots cool, then peel and slice. Cut slices into julienne and place in bowl. Season beetroots generously. Add onion and herbs to bowl.

4 Mix remaining ingredients together in small bowl and season well. Pour dressing over salad and toss.

5 Serve with fresh asparagus. Garnish with lemon quarters and fresh tarragon, if desired.

Salad of Fresh Beetroot and Chicory
(4 to 6 servings)

2	beetroots, boiled and peeled	2
1	large apple, cored and peeled	1
3	chicory heads, cored and cleaned	3
2	large potatoes, boiled and peeled	2
15 ml	chopped fresh parsley	1 tbsp
15 ml	chopped fresh chives	1 tbsp
75 ml	mayonnaise	2 1/2 fl oz
	salt and pepper	
	pinch of paprika	

1 Cut beetroots and apple into julienne. Place in large bowl.

2 Tear chicory leaves into small pieces and add to bowl.

3 Cut potatoes into cubes, add to bowl and toss ingredients.

4 Add fresh herbs, mayonnaise and seasonings. Mix well, correct seasoning and serve.

Cold Purée of Aubergine Salad
(4 servings)

2	aubergines	2
150 ml	olive oil	6 fl oz
75 ml	balsamic vinegar	2 ½ fl oz
2 ml	English mustard	½ tsp
	salt and freshly ground pepper	
	lemon juice to taste	
	lettuce leaves	

1 Preheat oven to 180°C (350°F) mark 4.

2 Place whole aubergines in roasting tin. Bake 40 minutes or adjust time according to size. Test if aubergines are done by piercing with knife. Flesh should be soft with no resistance.

3 When cooked, remove aubergines from oven and let cool. Peel, discard skin and purée flesh.

4 Add oil, vinegar and mustard. Mix well and season generously. Add lemon juice to taste.

5 Serve cold on lettuce leaves. Garnish with chicory, if desired.

Lamb Salad with Roasted Sweet Peppers
(4 to 6 servings)

1	sweet red pepper	1
1	sweet yellow pepper	1
450 g	leftover roast lamb, cut into julienne	1 lb
1	celery stick, thinly sliced	1
2	hard-boiled eggs, cut in wedges	2
3	bamboo shoots, sliced	3
75 ml	Ranch Dressing (see p. 95)	2 1/2 fl oz
30 g	toasted pine nuts	1 oz
	salt and pepper	
	lemon juice to taste	

1 Cut sweet peppers in half and remove seeds. Oil skin and place cut-side-down on baking sheet; grill 6 minutes. Remove and let cool. Peel off skin, slice peppers and place in large bowl.

2 Add lamb, celery, hard-boiled eggs and bamboo shoots to bowl. Season well and toss gently.

3 Add Ranch Dressing and mix well. Add lemon juice to taste and season with pepper. Mix again.

4 Serve salad on lettuce leaves and sprinkle with toasted pine nuts.

Fresh Seafood Salad
(4 servings)

1	head cabbage lettuce, washed and dried	1
2	tomatoes, peeled, seeded and diced	2
1	apple, cored, peeled and diced	1
1	cucumber, peeled, seeded and diced	1
200 g	cooked fresh crabmeat	7 oz
6	fresh prawns, cooked	6
50 ml	mayonnaise	2 fl oz
30 ml	soured cream	2 tbsp
15 ml	chopped fresh chives	1 tbsp
	salt and pepper	
	juice of 1 lemon	

1 Divide lettuce leaves among dinner plates. Set aside.

2 Place tomatoes, apple, cucumber and crabmeat in bowl. Peel, devein and cut cooked prawns in half. Add to bowl and season well.

3 Combine remaining ingredients in small bowl. Add to seafood and mix well. Season to taste.

4 Spoon seafood salad onto plates lined with lettuce leaves. Accompany with radishes if in season. Garnish with tomato wedges and lamb's lettuce, if desired.

Avocado, Grapefruit and Smoked Salmon Salad
(4 servings)

2	**grapefruits**	2
2	**avocados, stoned, peeled and diced**	2
225 g	**smoked salmon, sliced**	½ lb
15 ml	**French mustard**	1 tbsp
50 ml	**olive oil**	2 fl oz
	salt and freshly ground pepper	
	juice of 1½ lemons	
	romaine lettuce leaves	

1 Cut thin slice from top and bottom of grapefruits. Using a sharp knife to remove rind and white pith, trace contour of fruit. Hold fruit in one hand and cut between membranes to release sections of fruit. Place in bowl.

2 Add avocados and smoked salmon to bowl. Season generously with salt and pepper.

3 Mix mustard, oil, lemon juice, salt and pepper together in a separate bowl. Taste and add more oil if lemon is too strong.

4 Pour vinaigrette over salad, toss gently and serve on lettuce leaves.

Lamb's Lettuce and Escarole Salad
(4 servings)

1	head escarole	1
1	head endive	1
1	head lamb's lettuce	1
75 ml	double cream	2 1/2 fl oz
15 ml	French mustard	1 tbsp
	salt and freshly ground pepper	
	lemon juice to taste	

1 Wash greens in plenty of cold water and dry thoroughly. Tear leaves into small pieces and place in large bowl.

2 Mix cream and mustard together; season well. Add lemon juice to taste and pour dressing over greens. Toss and serve.

Roquefort Salad
(4 servings)

2	heads romaine lettuce, washed and dried	2
5	rashers crisp-cooked bacon	5
225 g	Roquefort cheese, crumbled	½ lb
30 ml	wine vinegar	2 tbsp
75 ml	olive oil	2½ fl oz
45 g	croutons	1½ oz
	salt and freshly ground pepper	
	juice of ½ lemon	
	few drops of Worcestershire sauce	

1 Tear lettuce leaves into small pieces and place in large bowl. Season generously. Chop bacon and toss with lettuce.

2 Place three-quarters of cheese in food processor. Add vinegar, oil, salt and pepper. Blend several seconds. Add lemon juice and Worcestershire sauce; blend again to combine.

3 Pour dressing over salad and mix well. Add remaining cheese and croutons. Toss and serve. Garnish with cherry tomatoes and parsley, if desired.

Salad Isabella
(4 to 6 servings)

225 g	fresh mushrooms, cleaned and thinly sliced	¹/₂ lb
2	celery sticks from celery heart	2
2	potatoes, boiled and peeled	2
225 g	French beans, cooked	¹/₂ lb
3	cooked artichoke bottoms, cut into julienne	3
15 ml	chopped fresh parsley	1 tbsp
	salt and pepper	
	Mustard Vinaigrette (see p. 86)	

Mustard Vinaigrette (see p. 86)

1 Place mushrooms in large bowl.

2 Slice celery sticks and potatoes into julienne. Add to bowl containing mushrooms.

3 Cut French beans into 2.5-cm (1-in) pieces. Add to bowl along with artichoke bottoms and parsley. Season well.

4 Pour vinaigrette over salad and mix well. Serve.

Romaine Salad with Warm Bacon Dressing
(4 to 6 servings)

75 ml	olive oil	2 ½ fl oz
5	rashers bacon, diced	5
1	red onion, peeled and sliced in rings	1
1	large head romaine lettuce, washed and dried	1
12	cherry tomatoes, halved	12
2	garlic cloves, peeled and thinly sliced	2
30 ml	balsamic vinegar	2 tbsp
30 g	grated Parmesan cheese	1 oz
	salt and freshly ground pepper	

1 Heat 15 ml (1 tbsp) oil in frying pan over medium heat. Add bacon and cook until crisp. Using slotted spoon, remove bacon and set aside.

2 Add red onion to hot bacon fat in pan. Cook 5 minutes over medium heat.

3 Tear lettuce into small pieces and place in large bowl. Add red onion and bacon. Pour in some of hot bacon fat. Toss quickly.

4 Add tomatoes, garlic and vinegar; mix well. Season generously and add remaining oil. Mix well and add cheese. Toss and serve.

German Potato Salad with Apple
(4 to 6 servings)

2	hard-boiled eggs	2
15 ml	French mustard	1 tbsp
1	shallot, peeled and chopped	1
45 ml	wine vinegar	3 tbsp
75 ml	olive oil	2½ fl oz
350 g	diced cooked potatoes	¾ lb
200 g	diced peeled apples	7 oz
3	gherkins, cut into julienne	3
15 ml	chopped fresh parsley	1 tbsp
	salt and freshly ground pepper	

1 Slice hard-boiled eggs in half and place yolks in bowl. Chop egg whites and set aside.

2 Mash egg yolks; incorporate mustard, shallot and vinegar. When combined, add oil and mix well. Season with salt and pepper.

3 Place potatoes, apple and gherkins in separate bowl. Add egg dressing and mix well. Add parsley and season generously; mix again.

4 Serve salad on lettuce leaves and decorate with chopped egg whites.

Warm Scallop and Prawn Salad
(4 servings)

4	garlic cloves, peeled, crushed and puréed	4
2	anchovy fillets, drained and puréed	2
75 ml	olive oil	2½ fl oz
12	fresh prawns, peeled, deveined and halved	12
30 g	croutons	1 oz
12	fresh large scallops, cleaned and halved	12
1	large head romaine lettuce, washed and dried	1
45 ml	grated Parmesan cheese	3 tbsp
	juice of 1 lemon	
	salt and pepper	

1 Place half of puréed garlic in bowl with anchovies; mix well. Add lemon juice and mix again. Add half of oil, season and blend well. Set aside.

2 Heat remaining oil in frying pan over medium heat. Add prawns and croutons; cook 2 minutes. Add scallops and remaining garlic; continue cooking 3 minutes.

3 Meanwhile, tear lettuce leaves into small pieces and place in large bowl. Arrange prawn and scallop mixture over lettuce. Add lemon vinaigrette and mix well.

4 Season, sprinkle with cheese and serve.

Citrus Fruit Salad with Avocado
(4 servings)

2	large ripe avocados	2
2	large grapefruits	2
3	oranges	3
75 ml	double cream	2 ½ fl oz
15 ml	soured cream	1 tbsp
5 ml	French mustard	1 tsp
	juice of ½ lemon	
	salt and white pepper	
	cayenne pepper to taste	
	fresh mint leaves	

1 Cut avocados in half, lengthways. Twist halves apart and remove stone. Peel and slice flesh and place in bowl.

2 Cut thin slice from top and bottom of grapefruits and oranges. Using a sharp knife to remove rind and white pith, trace contour of fruit. Hold fruit in one hand and cut between membranes to release sections of fruit. Add to bowl containing avocados.

3 Mix double cream with soured cream. Stir in mustard and lemon juice. Season with salt and both peppers.

4 Pour dressing over salad and mix well. Garnish portions with fresh mint leaves.

Marinated Tomato and Red Onion Salad
(4 servings)

1	sweet yellow pepper	1
4	large tomatoes, cored	4
1	red onion, peeled and sliced very thinly	1
5 ml	chopped fresh ginger	1 tsp
1 ml	ground ginger	1/4 tsp
2	garlic cloves, peeled and thinly sliced	2
	salt and freshly ground pepper	
	lemon juice	
	chopped chilli pepper to taste	

1 Cut sweet pepper in half and remove seeds. Oil skin and place cut-side-down on baking sheet; grill 6 minutes. Remove and let cool. Peel off skin, slice pepper and set aside.

2 Plunge tomatoes into saucepan with boiling water. Remove tomatoes after 1 minute or as soon as skins start to loosen. When cool enough to handle, peel off skins. Cut tomatoes in quarters and squeeze out seeds.

3 Place tomatoes in bowl and add onion; season well. Toss and set aside.

4 Place lemon juice, fresh and ground ginger and garlic in small bowl. Add chopped chilli pepper to taste and mix well.

5 Pour mixture over tomatoes and mix well. Marinate 2 hours at room temperature.

6 Serve marinated salad decorated with slices of roasted sweet pepper.

Fresh Fennel Salad
(4 servings)

1	large fennel bulb	1
60 ml	olive oil	4 tbsp
6	cooked artichoke hearts, halved	6
45 ml	lemon juice	3 tbsp
	salt and freshly ground pepper	

1 Remove leaves and stem from fennel bulb. Cut in half and peel. Cut each half, lengthways, into 3 pieces.

2 Place fennel in saucepan and pour in enough water to barely cover. Add 15 ml (1 tbsp) oil and season with salt. Cover and cook 30 minutes over low heat. When cooked, remove pan from cooker and let cool.

3 Place fennel and artichoke hearts on platter. Mix lemon juice with remaining oil and season well. Pour over salad. Garnish with spinach leaves, cherry tomatoes and fresh fennel, if desired.

Spring Salad with Lemon Dressing
(4 to 6 servings)

I	head romaine lettuce, washed and dried	I
I	head leaf lettuce, washed and dried	I
225 g	fresh mushrooms*, cleaned, sliced and blanched	½ lb
350 g	fresh asparagus, cooked and cut in 2.5-cm (1-in) pieces	¾ lb
12	radishes, cleaned and quartered	12
50 ml	double cream	2 fl oz
30 ml	mayonnaise	2 tbsp
2 ml	French mustard	½ tsp
5 ml	grated lemon rind	I tsp
	salt and pepper	
	juice of I lemon	

1 Tear lettuce leaves into small pieces and place in large bowl. Add mushrooms, asparagus and radishes. Season well.

2 Place cream, mayonnaise and mustard in small bowl. Mix together and season well. Add lemon rind and lemon juice; mix again.

3 Pour dressing over salad and toss. Correct seasoning and serve. Decorate salad with slices of hard-boiled egg, if desired.

* You may use whichever mushrooms are in season: shiitake, oyster, etc.

Russian Salad
(4 to 6 servings)

3	carrots, peeled and diced	3
3	potatoes, peeled and diced	3
1	small white turnip, peeled and diced	1
175 g	frozen green peas	6 oz
225 g	French beans	1/2 lb
250 ml	mayonnaise	8 fl oz
15 ml	chopped fresh parsley	1 tbsp
15 ml	chopped fresh chives	1 tbsp
	salt and pepper	
	lemon juice to taste	
	few drops of hot pepper sauce	

1 Cook all vegetables in boiling, salted water until tender. Drain thoroughly and place in bowl.

2 Season vegetables well and incorporate mayonnaise. Add lemon juice to taste and mix well.

3 Add fresh herbs and hot pepper sauce. Mix and correct seasoning.

4 Chill salad before serving.

Caesar Salad
(4 to 6 servings)

2	large heads romaine lettuce	2
I	garlic clove, peeled and halved	I
2	garlic cloves, blanched and puréed	2
6	anchovy fillets, drained and puréed	6
50 ml	olive oil	2 fl oz
I	large egg, coddled 2 minutes	I
45 g	croutons	I ½ oz
60 g	grated Parmesan cheese	2 oz
	juice of 2 lemons	
	salt and freshly ground pepper	

1 Separate lettuce into leaves and wash well in plenty of cold water. Drain and dry thoroughly. Tear leaves into small pieces and set aside.

2 Rub inside of wooden salad bowl with garlic halves. Discard garlic.

3 Place puréed garlic in salad bowl. Add anchovies and mix together. Mix in oil. Add lemon juice, season and mix well. Add coddled egg and incorporate with whisk.

4 Add lettuce to dressing in bowl. Toss until evenly coated. Season well and toss again.

5 Add croutons and cheese. Toss, season and serve.

Cucumber and Prawn Salad
(4 servings)

350 g	fresh prawns	³/₄ lb
1	head cabbage lettuce, washed and dried	1
1	large cucumber, peeled, seeded and sliced	1
15 ml	chopped fresh chives	1 tbsp
1	shallot, peeled and chopped	1
50 ml	extra virgin olive oil	2 fl oz
5 ml	chopped chilli pepper	1 tsp
	salt and pepper	

1 Place prawns in saucepan with cold water and bring to boil. Remove pan from heat and let prawns stand 3 minutes. Place pan under cold running water to stop cooking process. Drain prawns and peel. Using tip of paring knife, remove dark dorsal vein.

2 Arrange lettuce leaves on serving plates.

3 Place prawns in large bowl. Add remaining ingredients and mix well. Season to taste and serve over lettuce.

Lettuce and Carrot Salad with Chèvre
(4 servings)

1	head romaine lettuce, washed and dried	1
2	carrots, peeled and grated	2
1	apple, cored, peeled and diced large	1
30 ml	olive oil	2 tbsp
90 g	chèvre (goats' milk) cheese	3 oz
	juice of 1 ½ lemons	
	salt and pepper	

1 Tear lettuce into small pieces and place in bowl. Add carrots and apple. Squeeze in lemon juice and mix well.

2 Season generously and pour in oil; mix again. Add chèvre cheese, mix gently and serve.

3 Accompany with garlic bread, if desired.

Cucumber and Egg Salad
(4 to 6 servings)

3	cucumbers, sliced	3
15 ml	chopped fresh parsley	1 tbsp
2	hard-boiled eggs, chopped	2
	salt	
	olive oil and wine vinegar to taste	
	freshly ground pepper	
	radiccio leaves (optional)	

1 Spread cucumber slices on large serving platter. Sprinkle generously with salt and let stand 2 hours at room temperature. Rinse cucumbers under cold water and drain well.

2 Place cucumbers in deep serving platter. Add oil and vinegar to taste. Sprinkle with parsley and season with pepper.

3 Decorate centre of platter with radiccio leaves and hard-boiled eggs. Serve.

Simple Avocado Salad with Sesame Seeds

(4 servings)

30 ml	wine vinegar	2 tbsp
15 ml	French mustard	1 tbsp
90 ml	olive oil	3 fl oz
2	garlic cloves, peeled and halved	2
2	large ripe avocados	2
30 ml	toasted sesame seeds	2 tbsp
	lemon juice	
	red leaf lettuce leaves	

1 Place vinegar and mustard in bowl. Season well and add oil. Whisk together. Add garlic and let stand 15 minutes.

2 Meanwhile, cut avocados in half, lengthways. Twist halves apart and remove stone. Peel and slice flesh. Toss slices in lemon juice and arrange on lettuce leaves.

3 Remove garlic from vinaigrette and discard. Whisk in toasted sesame seeds and drizzle vinaigrette over avocados. Garnish with radiccio leaves and enoki mushrooms, if desired.

Quick Navy Bean and Lentil Salad
(4 to 6 servings)

I	sweet red pepper	I
90 g	tinned navy beans, drained	3 oz
100 g	tinned lentils, drained	3½ oz
½	red onion, thinly sliced	½
45 ml	red wine vinegar	3 tbsp
50 ml	olive oil	2 fl oz
15 ml	chopped fresh tarragon	I tbsp
	salt and pepper	

1 Cut sweet pepper in half and remove seeds. Oil skin and place cut-side-down on baking sheet; grill 6 minutes. Remove and let cool. Peel off skin, slice pepper and place in large bowl.

2 Add navy beans, lentils and red onion. Toss together.

3 Add remaining ingredients and mix well. Marinate 30 minutes at room temperature.

4 Add more oil or vinegar as desired, before serving.

Hot Lentil Salad with Bacon Dressing
(4 to 6 servings)

15 ml	olive oil	1 tbsp
5	rashers bacon, diced	5
½	red onion, roughly chopped	½
2	tomatoes, peeled, seeded and chopped (see p. 7)	2
1	garlic clove, peeled and sliced	1
45 ml	wine vinegar	3 tbsp
400 g	cooked lentils, still warm	14 oz
15 ml	chopped fresh basil	1 tbsp
45 ml	olive oil	3 tbsp
	salt and pepper	

1 Heat 15 ml (1 tbsp) oil in frying pan over medium heat. Add bacon and onion; cook until crisp. Transfer contents of pan to bowl.

2 Add tomatoes and garlic to hot pan. Continue cooking 3 minutes over medium heat. Pour in vinegar and cook 1 minute over high heat.

3 Add lentils to bacon and onion in bowl. Pour in hot dressing and mix well. Add remaining ingredients and mix again.

4 Correct seasoning and serve with garlic cheese bread, if desired.

Prawns and Mangetouts with Mixed Greens
(4 servings)

15 ml	soy sauce	1 tbsp
30 ml	dry white wine	2 tbsp
5 ml	sesame oil	1 tsp
1	garlic clove, peeled, crushed and chopped	1
30 ml	olive oil	2 tbsp
16	prawns, peeled and deveined	16
2	garlic cloves, peeled and thinly sliced	2
150 g	mangetouts	1/3 lb
1	small head radiccio, washed and dried	1
1	small bunch watercress, washed and dried	1
3	chicory heads, cored, washed and dried	3
	pinch of sugar	
	salt and pepper	

1 Mix soy sauce with white wine and sesame oil. Add chopped garlic and pinch of sugar. Mix again and set aside.

2 Heat olive oil in frying pan over medium heat. Add prawns and sliced garlic; season well. Cook 3 minutes over high heat, stirring once. Remove prawns from pan and set aside in large bowl.

3 Add mangetouts to hot pan and season well. Cook 3 minutes over high heat. Add to prawns in bowl.

4 Add radiccio leaves, watercress and chicory to bowl. Season generously and pour in soy dressing. Toss and serve with garlic bread, if desired.

Mixed Summer Vegetable Salad
(4 to 6 servings)

I	small head broccoli, in florets	I
I	small head cauliflower, in florets	I
225 g	French beans	½ lb
I	bunch fresh asparagus	I
I	carrot, peeled and sliced	I
75 ml	mayonnaise	2½ fl oz
50 ml	Ranch Dressing (see p. 95)	2 fl oz
10	slices salami, cut into julienne	10
15 ml	chopped fresh basil	I tbsp
15 ml	chopped fresh tarragon	I tbsp
	salt and pepper	

1 Blanch vegetables separately in boiling, salted water until just tender. Drain well.

2 Place blanched vegetables in large bowl and season well. Add mayonnaise and Ranch Dressing; mix well.

3 Add salami and fresh herbs. Mix lightly and serve.

Prawn and Lychee Nut Salad
(4 servings)

700 g	fresh prawns, cooked, peeled and deveined	1 ½ lb
2	ripe avocados, peeled, stoned and sliced	2
150 g	lychee nuts	5 oz
2	garlic cloves, peeled and sliced	2
30 ml	lemon juice	2 tbsp
30 ml	tarragon vinegar	2 tbsp
100 ml	olive oil	3 ½ fl oz
15 ml	chilli sauce	1 tbsp
	lettuce leaves	
	salt and freshly ground pepper	
	pinch of sugar	
	pinch of English mustard	
	pinch of paprika	
	lemon wedges	

1 Arrange lettuce leaves on serving platter. Fill platter with prawns and slices of avocado. Top with lychee nuts. Season well.

2 Place garlic, lemon juice, vinegar, oil and chilli sauce in small bowl. Mix well. Add all seasonings and mix again.

3 Drizzle sauce over prawns and avocados. Garnish with lemon wedges and serve.

Fancy Tuna Salad
(4 to 6 servings)

350 g	fresh tuna, poached and flaked	¾ lb
I	small cucumber, peeled, seeded and diced	I
I	celery stick, diced	I
3	spring onions, chopped	3
60 g	chopped pimiento pepper	2 oz
2	tomatoes, peeled, seeded and chopped	2
50 ml	mayonnaise	2 fl oz
15 ml	French mustard	I tbsp
15 ml	chopped fresh parsley	I tbsp
4	hard-boiled eggs, quartered	4
	salt and pepper	
	juice of I lemon	
	lettuce leaves	

1 Place tuna, cucumber, celery, spring onions, pimiento pepper and tomatoes in bowl. Season with salt and pepper.

2 Mix mayonnaise with mustard in separate bowl. Add to salad and mix well.

3 Add parsley and lemon juice; mix again. Correct seasoning and serve salad on lettuce leaves. Garnish with hard-boiled eggs.

Warm Cucumber Potato Salad with Brie Cheese

(4 servings)

2	cucumbers, peeled, seeded and sliced	2
2	large potatoes	2
¹/₂	red onion, peeled and sliced in rings	¹/₂
1	small head romaine lettuce, washed and dried	1
45 ml	red wine vinegar	3 tbsp
15 ml	chopped fresh parsley	1 tbsp
15 ml	chopped fresh chives	1 tbsp
50 ml	olive oil	2 fl oz
10	small slices of Brie cheese	10
	salt and pepper	

1 Spread sliced cucumbers on large platter. Sprinkle with salt and let stand 30 minutes at room temperature. Pour off liquid, rinse under cold water and drain well.

2 Meanwhile, boil potatoes in skins until cooked. Peel potatoes, slice and place in large bowl.

3 Add cucumbers and onion to potatoes. Tear lettuce leaves into small pieces and add to bowl. Season well.

4 Sprinkle in vinegar and fresh herbs. Toss, then pour in oil. Mix well. Correct seasoning and garnish portions with Brie cheese.

Tropical Fruit and Chicken Salad
(4 to 6 servings)

1	**ripe pineapple**	1
1	**orange**	1
1	**grapefruit**	1
1	**thick slice watermelon, diced**	1
2	**whole chicken breasts, cooked* and sliced**	2
50 ml	**mayonnaise**	2 fl oz
30 ml	**soured cream**	2 tbsp
	salt and freshly ground pepper	
	dash of paprika and cayenne pepper	

1 To prepare pineapple, slice off frond and stem end. Cut pineapple lengthways into quarters. Remove core from each quarter and discard. Cut off rind from quarters and dice flesh.

2 Cut thin slice from top and bottom of orange and grapefruit. Using a sharp knife to remove rind and white pith, trace contour of fruit. Hold fruit in one hand and cut between membranes to release sections of fruit.

3 Place all ingredients in bowl and toss together. Cover and marinate 1 hour in refrigerator.

4 Serve on romaine lettuce leaves and decorate with whole slices of lime and orange, if desired.

*Chicken may be grilled or barbecued.

Spicy Pepper Salad with Chickpeas
(4 to 6 servings)

1	sweet red pepper	1
1	sweet yellow pepper	1
1	sweet green pepper	1
160 g	tinned chickpeas, drained	5 1/2 oz
2	garlic cloves, peeled and thinly sliced	2
15 ml	wine vinegar	1 tbsp
45 ml	olive oil	3 tbsp
	salt and freshly ground pepper	
	crushed chillies to taste	
	juice of 1 lemon	

1 Cut sweet peppers in half and remove seeds. Oil skin and place cut-side-down on baking sheet; grill 6 minutes. Remove and let cool. Peel off skin, slice peppers and place in large bowl.

2 Add chickpeas and season well. Add remaining ingredients and mix well. Marinate 30 minutes before serving.

Classic Garden Tomato Salad
(4 to 6 servings)

5	ripe tomatoes*	5
2	shallots, peeled and finely chopped	2
15 ml	chopped fresh parsley	1 tbsp
	olive oil and red wine vinegar to taste	
	salt and freshly ground pepper	

1 Core tomatoes and cut into quarters. Place on large serving platter. Season generously with salt and pepper.

2 Sprinkle shallots and parsley over tomatoes. Add oil and vinegar to taste; mix well. Correct seasoning and marinate 30 minutes at room temperature. Add more oil and vinegar, if needed.

3 Serve at room temperature.

*You may also use yellow tomatoes, in season.

Steak and Beans in Salad
(4 servings)

30 ml	red wine vinegar	2 tbsp
15 ml	French mustard	1 tbsp
1	garlic clove, peeled, crushed and chopped	1
15 ml	chopped fresh tarragon	1 tbsp
125 ml	olive oil	4 fl oz
225 g	leftover cooked sirloin steak, sliced 1 cm (½ in) thick	½ lb
250 g	cooked white beans	9 oz
1	red leaf lettuce, washed and dried	1
2	hard-boiled eggs, sliced	2
	salt and pepper	
	chopped fresh parsley	

1 Place vinegar, mustard, salt and pepper in small bowl. Add garlic, tarragon and oil; whisk to incorporate.

2 Combine beef and beans. Season generously and add dressing. Mix well, cover and marinate 1 hour in refrigerator.

3 To serve salad, line plates with lettuce leaves. Add portions of beef and beans and decorate with sliced hard-boiled eggs. Sprinkle with chopped parsley and serve.

Rice Salad with Raisins and Toasted Nuts
(6 to 8 servings)

300 g	steamed white rice	11 oz
75 g	stoned black olives, chopped	2½ oz
60 g	diced pimiento pepper	2 oz
75 g	cooked green peas	2½ oz
60 g	sliced celery	2 oz
75 g	golden seedless raisins	2½ oz
75 g	toasted pine nuts	2½ oz
125 ml	Basic Vinaigrette (see p. 89)	4 fl oz
4	hard-boiled eggs	4
75 ml	mayonnaise	2½ fl oz
	salt and black pepper	
	cayenne pepper	
	lemon juice	
	fresh parsley sprigs	

1 Place rice, olives, pimiento pepper and green peas in large bowl. Add celery, raisins and pine nuts.

2 Season generously with salt, black pepper and cayenne pepper. Pour in vinaigrette and toss well. Mix in lemon juice to taste.

3 Spoon salad onto dinner plates. Slice hard-boiled eggs carefully. Arrange slices overlapping on rice salad. Add dollop of mayonnaise. Decorate plates with parsley sprigs and serve.

Hot Chicken Salad with Raspberry Vinaigrette
(4 servings)

1	large head romaine lettuce, washed and dried	1
1	head radiccio, washed and dried	1
50 ml	olive oil	2 fl oz
2	garlic cloves, peeled, crushed and chopped	2
2	shallots, peeled and chopped	2
1	whole chicken breast, cooked and thinly sliced	1
30 ml	raspberry wine vinegar	2 tbsp
45 g	croutons	1½ oz
30 g	toasted pine nuts	1 oz
15 ml	chopped fresh basil	1 tbsp
15 ml	chopped fresh parsley	1 tbsp
	salt and pepper	
	lemon juice to taste	

1 Tear romaine and radiccio leaves into small pieces and arrange on serving platter.

2 Heat half of oil in frying pan over medium heat. Add garlic, shallots and sliced chicken. Season and cook 2 minutes over high heat.

3 Add vinegar, mix well and cook 1 minute over low heat. Place over lettuce.

4 Add remaining oil to pan. When hot, add croutons, pine nuts and herbs. Cook 2 minutes over high heat. Add to salad.

5 Season salad well and sprinkle with lemon juice. Serve.

Celeriac Rémoulade
(4 servings)

1	celeriac	1
175 ml	mayonnaise	6 fl oz
5 ml	French mustard	1 tsp
15 ml	chopped fresh parsley	1 tbsp
5 ml	basil	1 tsp
1	gherkin, cut into julienne	1
30 ml	capers	2 tbsp
	salt and pepper	

1 Place celeriac in boiling, salted water. Blanch 6 minutes or adjust time according to size. Remove celeriac, peel and cut into fine julienne.

2 Place celeriac in bowl with remaining ingredients. Mix together and correct seasoning.

3 Serve on greens of your choice (e.g. leaf lettuce, lamb's lettuce, endive) and accompany with Italian salami, if desired.

Cauliflower and Avocado Salad
(4 to 6 servings)

1	cauliflower	1
3	beetroots, boiled, peeled and sliced	3
1	avocado, peeled, halved, stoned and sliced	1
	salt and pepper	
	Tomato Vinaigrette (see p. 90)	

1 Wash cauliflower and remove dark leaves at stem end. Place cauliflower, core-side-down, in pot with boiling, salted water. Blanch 5 minutes. Drain and cool under cold water.

2 Divide cauliflower into florets and place in salad bowl. Add beetroots and avocado; season well.

3 Pour in Tomato Vinaigrette and mix well. Marinate 30 minutes at room temperature before serving.

Brittany Salad
(4 to 6 servings)

2	courgettes	2
3	large tomatoes, cored	3
4	cooked artichoke bottoms, sliced	4
225 g	fresh prawns, peeled, deveined and cooked (see technique)	½ lb
2	hard-boiled eggs, sliced	2
	salt and freshly ground pepper	
	Mustard Vinaigrette (see p. 86)	
	lettuce leaves	

1 Cut courgettes into slices 1 cm (½ in) thick. Cook 2 minutes in boiling, salted water. Remove using slotted spoon and set aside to drain. Pat dry with absorbent kitchen paper.

2 Plunge tomatoes into boiling water just long enough to loosen skins. Remove, let cool and peel. Cut tomatoes into wedges.

3 Place all vegetables and prawns in large bowl; season well. Pour in vinaigrette and mix well. Correct seasoning.

4 Serve salad on lettuce leaves and decorate with slices of hard-boiled egg.

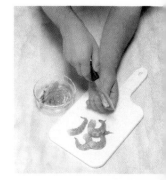

Picnic Salad
(4 to 6 servings)

2	potatoes, boiled, peeled and diced	2
250 g	cooked white beans	9 oz
75 g	stoned black olives	2½ oz
2	garlic cloves, peeled, crushed and chopped	2
15 ml	wine vinegar	1 tbsp
50 ml	olive oil	2 fl oz
200 g	tinned tuna, drained and flaked	7 oz
15 ml	chopped fresh basil	1 tbsp
15 ml	chopped fresh parsley	1 tbsp
	salt and freshly ground pepper	
	juice of 1 lemon	
	radiccio, washed and dried	

1 Place potatoes, white beans, olives and garlic in large bowl. Season generously. Add lemon juice and vinegar; blend well.

2 Pour in oil and mix well. Add tuna and fresh herbs; mix again. Correct seasoning and serve on bed of radiccio.

Cucumber and Bocconcini Cheese Salad
(4 to 6 servings)

3	cucumbers, peeled, seeded and diced	3
225 g	Bocconcini cheese, cubed	½ lb
3	spring onions, chopped	3
12	radishes, washed and sliced	12
175 ml	soured cream	6 fl oz
15 ml	tarragon vinegar	1 tbsp
30 ml	chopped dill pickle	2 tbsp
5 ml	French mustard	1 tsp
2	garlic cloves, blanched and puréed	2
15 ml	extra virgin olive oil	1 tbsp
	salt and pepper	
	pinch of paprika	

1 Spread diced cucumbers on large platter. Sprinkle with salt and let stand 2 hours at room temperature. Pour off liquid, rinse under cold water and drain well.

2 Place cucumbers in bowl with cheese, spring onions and radishes. Season well, cover and refrigerate 1 hour.

3 Mix remaining ingredients together in small bowl. Add to salad and mix well. Correct seasoning and serve.

Mediterranean Pasta Salad
(4 to 6 servings)

3	garlic cloves, blanched and puréed	3
15 ml	French mustard	1 tbsp
30 ml	balsamic vinegar	2 tbsp
90 ml	olive oil	3 fl oz
350 g	pasta, cooked	¾ lb
15 g	sun-dried tomatoes, chopped	½ oz
4	cooked artichoke hearts, quartered	4
175 g	cooked white beans	6 oz
12	slices Italian salami, cut into julienne	12
90 g	mozzarella cheese, diced	3 oz
	salt and freshly ground pepper	
	fresh chopped herbs in season	

1 Place garlic and mustard in small bowl; season well. Add vinegar and mix well. Whisk in oil and correct seasoning.

2 Place pasta, sun-dried tomatoes, artichoke hearts and white beans in large bowl. Pour in dressing and mix well. Season generously.

3 Add salami and cheese; mix again. Sprinkle with chopped fresh herbs in season and serve.

Chickpeas with Julienne of Salami
(4 to 6 servings)

300 g	tinned chickpeas, drained	11 oz
5	slices salami, cut into julienne	5
75 g	stoned black olives	2½ oz
½	sweet green pepper, thinly sliced	½
2	spring onions, chopped	2
60 g	pimiento pepper, chopped	2 oz
15 ml	olive oil	1 tbsp
	salt and pepper	
	few drops of Tabasco sauce	
	juice of 1 large lemon	

1 Place all ingredients, except oil and lemon juice, in large bowl.

2 Mix in oil and lemon juice. Correct seasoning, cover and marinate 2 hours in refrigerator.

3 Serve salad on lettuce leaves. Garnish with lemon slices and fresh sage, if desired.

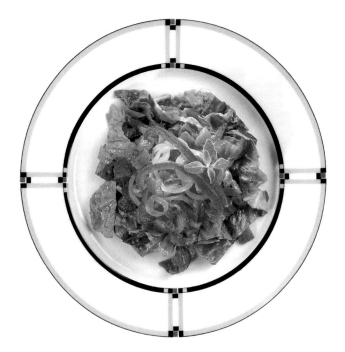

Wilted Greens in Salad
(4 servings)

1	head romaine lettuce, washed and dried	1
1	head escarole, washed and dried	1
15 ml	olive oil	1 tbsp
5	rashers bacon	5
1	red onion, peeled and sliced in rings	1
1	sweet red pepper, thinly sliced	1
2	tomatoes, peeled, seeded and cubed	2
2	garlic cloves, peeled and thinly sliced	2
45 ml	tomato sauce	3 tbsp
15 ml	French mustard	1 tbsp
	salt and freshly ground pepper	
	few drops hot pepper sauce	
	juice of 1 lemon	

1 Tear greens into small pieces and place in large bowl.

2 Heat oil in frying pan over medium heat. Add bacon and cook until crisp. Remove bacon from pan and set aside to drain on absorbent kitchen paper.

3 Add red onion rings to hot pan and cook 4 minutes over high heat. Add sweet pepper, tomatoes and garlic; continue cooking 2 minutes.

4 Pour hot vegetables over greens and toss quickly; season well. Crumble bacon and sprinkle over salad.

5 Mix tomato sauce and mustard together. Add hot pepper sauce and lemon juice. Pour over salad, toss and serve.

Warm Chicken Liver Salad

(4 servings)

1	large head leaf lettuce, washed and dried	1
75 ml	olive oil	2 ¹/₂ fl oz
3	rashers bacon, diced	3
225 g	chicken livers, cleaned and sliced	¹/₂ lb
2	garlic cloves, peeled, crushed and chopped	2
2	shallots, peeled and chopped	2
30 ml	balsamic vinegar	2 tbsp
15 ml	chopped fresh chives	1 tbsp
45 g	croutons	1 ¹/₂ oz
	salt and freshly ground pepper	

1 Tear lettuce leaves into small pieces and place in large bowl.

2 Heat 15 ml (1 tbsp) oil in frying pan over high heat. Add bacon and cook until crisp. Remove bacon and add to lettuce in bowl.

3 Add half of remaining oil to pan and heat. Add chicken livers and season well. Cook 2 minutes over medium-high heat. Add to salad bowl.

4 Add remaining oil to pan. When hot, add garlic and shallots; cook 1 minute over medium heat. Pour in vinegar and cook 20 seconds.

5 Pour mixture over salad and mix well. Add chives and croutons. Correct seasoning, toss and serve.

Cold Roast Beef Salad
(4 servings)

450 g	roast beef, cut into julienne	1 lb
1	sweet red pepper, cut into julienne	1
1	celery stick, thinly sliced	1
225 g	French beans, cooked and halved	½ lb
1	large tomato, peeled, seeded and cut into julienne	1
15 ml	chopped fresh parsley	1 tbsp
15 ml	chopped fresh basil	1 tbsp
45 ml	balsamic vinegar	3 tbsp
100 ml	olive oil	3½ fl oz
	salt and pepper	
	few drops of Tabasco sauce	

1 Place roast beef and vegetables in large bowl. Add fresh herbs and remaining ingredients.

2 Mix well and correct seasoning. Cover and marinate 30 minutes in refrigerator before serving.

3 Serve on lettuce leaves, if desired, and garnish with fresh herbs.

Greek Salad
(4 to 6 servings)

1	large head romaine lettuce, washed and dried	1
1	head red leaf lettuce, washed and dried	1
1	small red onion, peeled and sliced in rings	1
1	sweet green pepper, thinly sliced	1
1	sweet red pepper, thinly sliced	1
2	tomatoes, cored and cut in wedges	2
75 g	Greek olives	2½ oz
100 g	feta cheese, cubed	3½ oz
30 ml	wine vinegar	2 tbsp
30 ml	lemon juice	2 tbsp
2	garlic cloves, peeled, crushed and chopped	2
5 ml	oregano	1 tsp
75 ml	olive oil	2½ fl oz
	salt and freshly ground pepper	
	fresh herbs in season	

1 Tear lettuce leaves into small pieces and place in large bowl. Add red onion, sweet peppers, tomatoes, olives and cheese. Season with salt and pepper.

2 Place vinegar, lemon juice, garlic and oregano in small bowl. Season with salt and pepper. Add oil and whisk to incorporate.

3 Pour dressing over salad, mix well and garnish portions with fresh herbs, if desired.

Salad Aida
(4 servings)

1	head endive	1
1	head radiccio	1
2	tomatoes, cored and cut in wedges	2
2	cooked artichoke bottoms, sliced	2
1	sweet green pepper, sliced	1
	salt and freshly ground pepper	
	Mustard Vinaigrette (see p. 86)	
	lemon juice to taste	

1 Wash endive and radiccio in plenty of cold water. Dry thoroughly and tear leaves into small pieces. Place in large bowl with tomatoes.

2 Add artichoke bottoms and green pepper to bowl. Season well and pour in vinaigrette. Toss and add lemon juice to taste. Mix well, correct seasoning and serve.

Curried Prawn and Rice Salad
(6 servings)

185 g	long grain rice, rinsed	6½ oz
15 ml	olive oil	1 tbsp
350 g	fresh prawns, peeled and deveined	¾ lb
1	sweet red pepper, diced	1
1	celery stick, diced	1
4	slices cantaloupe, peeled and diced	4
25 ml	curry powder	1½ tbsp
2	garlic cloves, blanched and puréed	2
30 ml	wine vinegar	2 tbsp
90 ml	olive oil	3 fl oz
75 ml	plain yogurt	2½ fl oz
45 ml	chutney	3 tbsp
	salt and pepper	
	chopped fresh parsley	

1 Steam rice for 40 minutes. Season well and set aside to cool.

2 Heat 15 ml (1 tbsp) oil in frying pan over medium heat. Add prawns and cook 4 minutes, stirring during cooking. Add sweet pepper and continue cooking 1 minute.

3 Transfer prawns and sweet pepper to large bowl. Add rice, celery and cantaloupe. Season generously and mix.

4 Place curry powder, garlic, vinegar and remaining oil in small bowl. Season well and whisk together. Pour over salad and mix well.

5 Stir in yogurt and chutney. Correct seasoning, sprinkle with parsley and serve.

Plain Red Cabbage Salad
(4 to 6 servings)

I	head red cabbage, cored and shredded	I
50 ml	cider vinegar	2 fl oz
90 ml	olive oil	3 fl oz
12	black peppercorns	12
	pickling spices	
	salt and pepper	

1 Blanch cabbage 3 minutes in boiling, salted water. Cool under cold, running water and drain well. Place in bowl.

2 Place remaining ingredients in saucepan. Cook 3 minutes over medium heat.

3 Pour hot dressing over cabbage and season generously. If necessary, add more oil and vinegar. Marinate 3 hours before serving.

Black Bean Salad
(4 servings)

350 g	cooked black beans	¾ lb
½	red onion, peeled and chopped	½
1	celery stick, diced	1
2	tomatoes, peeled, seeded and chopped	2
2	garlic cloves, peeled, crushed and chopped	2
15 ml	chopped fresh parsley	1 tbsp
45 ml	balsamic vinegar	3 tbsp
90 ml	olive oil	3 fl oz
15 ml	grain mustard	1 tbsp
	salt and freshly ground pepper	

1 Place beans and vegetables in bowl. Add garlic, parsley and vinegar. Mix well.

2 Add remaining ingredients and mix again. Correct seasoning, cover and marinate 30 minutes in refrigerator before serving.

Tossed Green Salad
(6 servings)

1	small head cabbage lettuce	1
1	small leaf lettuce	1
2	chicory heads, cored	2
1	small radiccio lettuce, cored	1
1	garlic clove, peeled and halved	1
45 ml	olive oil	3 tbsp
30 ml	lemon juice	2 tbsp
5 ml	French mustard	1 tsp
15 ml	chopped fresh parsley	1 tbsp
	salt and freshly ground pepper	

1 Wash all lettuce in plenty of cold water and dry thoroughly.

2 Rub sides of wooden salad bowl with cut side of garlic; discard garlic. Tear lettuce leaves into small pieces and place in bowl. Season with salt and pepper.

3 Place oil, lemon juice and mustard in small bowl. Season well and add parsley. Whisk together and pour over salad. Toss, correct seasoning and serve.

Cooking Mushrooms for Salads

450 g	fresh mushrooms, cleaned	1 lb
125 ml	dry white wine	4 fl oz
5 ml	olive oil	1 tsp
1	bay leaf	1
	salt and pepper	
	lemon juice	

1 Place mushrooms and remaining ingredients in saucepan. Pour in enough cold water to 3/4 cover mushrooms. Cover with grease-proof paper touching surface of mushrooms and bring to boil.

2 Reduce heat to low and cook mushrooms 6 to 8 minutes.

3 Remove pan from heat and let mushrooms cool in liquid. Drain well before using.

4 If desired, mushrooms can be stored for later use. Keep in cooking liquid, cover tightly and refrigerate for up to a day.

Cooked Salad Dressing
(4 to 6 servings)

5 ml	sugar	1 tsp
30 ml	flour	2 tbsp
30 ml	water	2 tbsp
10 ml	English mustard	2 tsp
50 ml	white vinegar	2 fl oz
125 ml	water	4 fl oz
2	eggs, beaten	2
15 ml	soft butter	1 tbsp
	salt and pepper	
	few drops of Tabasco sauce	
	cold milk	

1 Place sugar, flour, salt and pepper in bowl. Add 30 ml (2 tbsp) water and mix together with whisk. Add mustard, vinegar and 125 ml (4 fl oz) water; incorporate with whisk.

2 Transfer mixture to saucepan and cook 3 minutes over low heat, stirring constantly. Remove pan from heat.

3 Incorporate eggs and butter, whisking until smooth.

4 Pour mixture into top part of double boiler. Cook 2 minutes over low heat, mixing constantly. Season with Tabasco sauce.

5 Transfer dressing to bowl and let cool. Thin with cold milk to reach desired consistency. Serve over lettuce and vegetable salads.

Homemade Mayonnaise
(8 to 10 servings)

2	egg yolks	2
15 ml	French mustard	1 tbsp
300 ml	olive oil	¹/₂ pt
15 ml	lemon juice or white vinegar	1 tbsp
	salt and pepper	

1 Place egg yolks in bowl. Add salt, pepper and mustard. Whisk together for 1 minute.

2 When egg yolks thicken, begin adding oil drop by drop. It is important to whisk constantly. As mixture thickens, increase flow of oil to thin stream. Taste mayonnaise and add more oil if desired.

3 Whisk in lemon juice or vinegar. Correct seasoning.

4 To store mayonnaise, stir in 15 ml (1 tbsp) of hot water. Cover with cling film touching surface and refrigerate for up to 3 days.

Mustard Vinaigrette
(6 to 8 servings)

1	egg yolk	1
15 ml	French mustard	1 tbsp
1	shallot, peeled and chopped	1
50 ml	balsamic vinegar	2 fl oz
250 ml	olive oil	8 fl oz
15 ml	chopped fresh parsley	1 tbsp
	salt and black pepper	
	few drops of lemon juice	
	cayenne pepper to taste	

1 Place egg yolk and mustard in bowl. Add shallot and vinegar; season well.

2 Incorporate oil in thin stream, whisking constantly. Add a few drops of lemon juice and cayenne pepper to taste. Add parsley.

This vinaigrette keeps well in a container with tight-fitting lid. Refrigerate for up to 3 days.

Mayonnaise with Fresh Tomato
(6 to 8 servings)

5 ml	olive oil	1 tsp
2	medium tomatoes, cored and diced	2
1	garlic clove, peeled, crushed and chopped	1
1	shallot, peeled and chopped	1
5 ml	tarragon	1 tsp
375 ml	Homemade Mayonnaise (see p. 85)	12 fl oz
	salt and pepper	
	pinch of crushed chillies	

1 Heat oil in frying pan over medium heat. Add tomatoes, garlic, shallot and all seasonings. Cook 12 minutes over medium heat.

2 Pass tomato mixture through vegetable mill or blender. Place purée in bowl and set aside to cool.

3 Add 50 ml (2 fl oz) or more of tomato mixture to Homemade Mayonnaise. Correct seasoning and serve with a variety of salads.

Tapenade
(4 to 6 servings)

135 g	stoned black olives	4 1/2 oz
4	anchovy fillets, drained and chopped	4
45 ml	lemon juice	3 tbsp
175 ml	olive oil	6 fl oz
	salt and pepper	

1 Place olives and anchovies in food processor; purée. Transfer mixture to bowl and stir in lemon juice.

2 Add oil and whisk to incorporate. Season well with salt and pepper.

Use tapenade as a condiment for fresh vegetables, cold meats and fish.

Light Chilli Mayonnaise
(4 to 6 servings)

125 ml	mayonnaise	4 fl oz
30 ml	buttermilk	2 tbsp
2	garlic cloves, blanched and puréed	2
15 ml	chilli sauce	1 tbsp
	salt and pepper	
	lemon juice to taste	

1 Mix all ingredients together in small bowl. Correct seasoning and serve.

Basic Vinaigrette
(4 to 6 servings)

30 ml	white or red wine vinegar	2 tbsp
90 ml	olive oil	3 fl oz
5 ml	chopped fresh parsley (optional)	1 tsp
5 ml	chopped fresh tarragon (optional)	1 tsp
5 ml	chopped fresh chives (optional)	1 tsp
	salt and freshly ground pepper	

1 Place vinegar in bowl. Add salt and pepper.

2 Add oil and whisk to incorporate. Add herbs, if using, and mix well.

3 Correct seasoning and serve.

Use this vinaigrette over green salads.

Tomato Vinaigrette
(6 to 8 servings)

2	garlic cloves, peeled and sliced	2
45 ml	lemon juice	3 tbsp
45 ml	wine vinegar	3 tbsp
125 ml	olive oil	4 fl oz
2 ml	sugar	½ tsp
30 ml	tomato sauce	2 tbsp
1 ml	English mustard	¼ tsp
15 ml	chopped fresh parsley	1 tbsp
	pepper	

1 In mixing bowl, combine all ingredients. Cover and marinate 1 hour in refrigerator.

2 Remove garlic before using. Serve over vegetable salads.

Soy Sauce Salad Dressing
(4 to 6 servings)

60 g	cottage cheese	2 oz
50 ml	soured cream	2 fl oz
125 ml	buttermilk	4 fl oz
15 ml	French mustard	1 tbsp
5 ml	wine vinegar	1 tsp
2 ml	soy sauce	½ tsp
	salt and pepper	
	few drops of Tabasco sauce	
	few drops of Worcestershire sauce	

1 Place all ingredients in food processor. Blend together and correct seasoning.

2 Refrigerate for up to 3 days, covered, until ready to use.

Cottage Cheese Blender Dressing
(4 to 6 servings)

135 g	cottage cheese	4 ½ oz
125 ml	mayonnaise	4 fl oz
50 ml	plain yogurt	2 fl oz
2	garlic cloves, blanched and puréed	2
5 ml	French mustard	I tsp
15 ml	white vinegar	I tbsp
	pinch of sugar	
	few drops of lemon juice	
	few drops of Tabasco sauce	
	salt and pepper	

1 Place cottage cheese in food processor and purée. Add remaining ingredients and blend until incorporated.

2 Correct seasoning and serve with vegetable salads.

Sauce Rémoulade
(serves 6 to 8)

375 ml	Homemade Mayonnaise (see p. 85)	12 fl oz
30 ml	French mustard	2 tbsp
30 ml	capers	2 tbsp
1	large pickle, finely chopped	1
15 ml	chopped fresh parsley	1 tbsp
15 ml	chopped fresh tarragon	1 tbsp
2	anchovy fillets, drained and chopped	2
¼	sweet yellow pepper, steamed, skinned and chopped	¼
	few drops of Tabasco sauce	
	freshly ground pepper	

1 Place all ingredients in bowl. Mix together until well blended. Correct seasoning and chill before serving.

A classic French sauce, rémoulade accompanies cold meats, fish, shellfish and egg dishes.

Tartar Sauce
(6 to 8 servings)

375 ml	Homemade Mayonnaise (see p. 85)	12 fl oz
2	hard-boiled eggs, diced	2
15 ml	capers	1 tbsp
1	pickle, finely chopped	1
5 ml	chopped fresh parsley	1 tsp
5 ml	chopped fresh chives	1 tsp
1	shallot, peeled and chopped	1
	salt and black pepper	
	cayenne pepper to taste	
	lemon juice to taste	

1 Mix all ingredients together until well blended.

Serve with cold or hot fish salads.

Thick Egg Vinaigrette
(4 to 6 servings)

15 ml	French mustard	1 tbsp
1	egg yolk	1
30 ml	wine vinegar	2 tbsp
90 ml	olive oil	3 fl oz
2	blanched garlic cloves, puréed	2
30 ml	soured cream	2 tbsp
	salt and pepper	
	lemon juice to taste	

1 Place mustard, egg yolk, salt and pepper in small bowl. Whisk together. Add vinegar and mix again.

2 Pour in oil and whisk until vinaigrette becomes thick. Mix in garlic and soured cream. Season well.

3 Add lemon juice to taste and serve.

Blue Cheese Dressing
(4 to 6 servings)

75 ml	plain yogurt	2 1/2 fl oz
45 g	cottage cheese	1 1/2 oz
125 ml	light mayonnaise	4 fl oz
60 g	crumbled blue cheese	2 oz
	few drops of Worcestershire sauce	
	few drops of lemon juice	
	salt and freshly ground pepper	
	pinch of paprika	

1 Mix all ingredients, except blue cheese, together until smooth.

2 Season well and add blue cheese. Mix and serve over lettuce.

Light Mayonnaise for Vegetable Salads
(4 to 6 servings)

75 ml	mayonnaise	2 1/2 fl oz
15 ml	soured cream	1 tbsp
5 ml	French mustard	1 tsp
15 ml	chopped fresh chives	1 tbsp
	salt and black pepper	
	cayenne pepper to taste	
	juice of 1/2 lemon	

1 Mix all ingredients together in small bowl. Correct seasoning and serve.

Ranch Dressing
(4 to 6 servings)

2	garlic cloves, blanched	2
250 ml	buttermilk	8 fl oz
175 ml	mayonnaise	6 fl oz
2 ml	celery seeds	½ tsp
5 ml	dill weed	1 tsp
2 ml	English mustard	½ tsp
	lemon juice to taste	
	salt and pepper	
	pinch of paprika	

1 To blanch garlic cloves, cook in boiling water for about 4 minutes. Remove cloves from water and let cool; peel and purée.

2 Place all ingredients in food processor; blend until smooth. Correct seasoning and serve.

Index